THE TWO WORLDS OF CHARLIE F.

Small Cast Adaptation

by Owen Sheers

‖SAMUEL FRENCH‖

Copyright © 2018 by Owen Sheers
All Rights Reserved

THE TWO WORLDS OF CHARLIE F. is fully protected under the copyright laws of the British Commonwealth, including Canada, the United States of America, and all other countries of the Copyright Union. All rights, including professional and amateur stage productions, recitation, lecturing, public reading, motion picture, radio broadcasting, television, online/digital production, and the rights of translation into foreign languages are strictly reserved.

ISBN 978-0-573-11637-7

www.concordtheatricals.co.uk
www.concordtheatricals.com

FOR AMATEUR PRODUCTION ENQUIRIES

UNITED KINGDOM AND WORLD
EXCLUDING NORTH AMERICA
licensing@concordtheatricals.co.uk
020-7054-7200
Each title is subject to availability from Concord Theatricals,
depending upon country of performance.

CAUTION: Professional and amateur producers are hereby warned that *THE TWO WORLDS OF CHARLIE F.* is subject to a licensing fee. The purchase, renting, lending or use of this book does not constitute a licence to perform this title(s), which licence must be obtained from the appropriate agent prior to any performance. Performance of this title(s) without a licence is a violation of copyright law and may subject the producer and/or presenter of such performances to penalties. Both amateurs and professionals considering a production are strongly advised to apply to the appropriate agent before starting rehearsals, advertising, or booking a theatre. A licensing fee must be paid whether the title is presented for charity or gain and whether or not admission is charged.

This work is published by Samuel French, an imprint of Concord Theatricals. Ltd

The Professional Rights in this play are controlled by Sayle Screen Ltd, 11 Jubilee Place, London SW3 3TD.

No one shall make any changes in this title for the purpose of production. No part of this book may be reproduced, stored in a retrieval system, scanned, uploaded, or transmitted in any form, by any means, now known or yet to be invented, including mechanical, electronic, digital, photocopying, recording, videotaping, or otherwise, without the prior written permission of the publisher. No one shall share this title, or part of this title, to any social media or file hosting websites.

The moral right of Owen Sheers to be identified as author of this work has been asserted in accordance with Section 77 of the Copyright, Designs and Patents Act 1988.

USE OF COPYRIGHTED MUSIC

A licence issued by Concord Theatricals to perform this play does not include permission to use the incidental music specified in this publication. In the United Kingdom: Where the place of performance is already licensed by the PERFORMING RIGHT SOCIETY (PRS) a return of the music used must be made to them. If the place of performance is not so licensed then application should be made to PRS for Music (www.prsformusic.com). A separate and additional licence from PHONOGRAPHIC PERFORMANCE LTD (www.ppluk.com) may be needed whenever commercial recordings are used. Outside the United Kingdom: Please contact the appropriate music licensing authority in your territory for the rights to any incidental music.

USE OF COPYRIGHTED THIRD-PARTY MATERIALS

Licensees are solely responsible for obtaining formal written permission from copyright owners to use copyrighted third-party materials (e.g., artworks, logos) in the performance of this play and are strongly cautioned to do so. If no such permission is obtained by the licensee, then the licensee must use only original materials that the licensee owns and controls. Licensees are solely responsible and liable for clearances of all third-party copyrighted materials, and shall indemnify the copyright owners of the play(s) and their licensing agent, Concord Theatricals Ltd., against any costs, expenses, losses and liabilities arising from the use of such copyrighted third-party materials by licensees.

IMPORTANT BILLING AND CREDIT REQUIREMENTS

If you have obtained performance rights to this title, please refer to your licensing agreement for important billing and credit requirements.

THE TWO WORLDS OF CHARLIE F. (small cast) is an adaptation of the original production first performed at the Theatre Royal Haymarket on 22nd January 2012. Directed by Stephen Rayne, produced by Alice Driver of Masterclass theatre for the Theatre Royal Haymarket, music by Jason Carr, design by Anthony Lamble, lighting and projection design by Will Reynolds, sound by Colin Pink and choreography by Lilly Phillips. The cast was as follows:

CHARLIE FOWLER .... Cassidy Little

NURSE/ YOUNG SIMI/ MICHELLE TAYLOR/
DANCER 2/ COMMON ROOM NURSE .... Teri Ann Bobb Baxter

BRITISH OFFICER .... Stewart Hill

CHARLIE'S MOTHER/ SARAH THOMAS/ TRACY BOOTH/
MARIE WARD/ COMMON ROOM NURSE................... Miriam Cooper

LAUREN PRESTON/ DANCER 1/
COMMON ROOM NURSE .... Lily Phillips

DAVID PHILLIPS/ PSYCHOLOGIST/ SINGING TEACHER/
DELIVERY MAN/ BUSINESSMAN 1 .... Owen Oldroyd

JEAN BARKER/ WAITRESS................................Venetia Maitland

JOHN BOOTH .... Tom Colley

DANIEL THOMAS.. Stewart Hill

ROGER SMITH .... Steve Shaw

LEROY JENKINS .... Dan Shaw

CHRIS WARD...Swifty

ALI BRIGGS ....Ash Young

SIMI YEATS.. Mauellia Simpson

DARREN SOBEY... Gareth Crabbe

FRANK TAYLOR/ BUSINESSMAN 2 ....Tomos Eames

CHARACTERS

CHARLIE FOWLER
NURSE
BRITISH OFFICER
CHARLIE'S MOTHER
LAUREN PRESTON
DAVID PHILLIPS
JEAN BARKER
JOHN BOOTH
DANIEL THOMAS
ROGER SMITH
LEROY JENKINS
CHRIS WARD
ALI BRIGGS
SIMI YEATS
YOUNG SIMI
DARREN SOBEY
FRANK TAYLOR
MICHELLE TAYLOR
SARAH THOMAS
TRACY BOOTH
MARIE WARD
PSYCHOLOGIST
SINGING TEACHER
DELIVERY MAN
BUSINESSMAN 1
BUSINESSMAN 2
DANCER 1
DANCER 2
WAITRESS
COMMON ROOM NURSES

NOTE FROM THE COMPOSER

For the original 2012 production of The Two Worlds of Charlie F by the Bravo 22 company, the songs were mostly (but not exclusively) performed to backing tracks, orchestrated to reflect the different styles (military band for the Training Song, and something more contemporary for the Pharmacopeia). I played piano live for a few moments, and one of the cast played a treble recorder solo in the Letters song. I would encourage you to use any musical talents in your acting company, and to feel free arrange the music in a manner appropriate to your production.

Jason Carr, 2021

ACT ONE

Scene One – Waking

Footage of **SOLDIERS**' *boots on patrol is projected onto gauze.*

Lights fade.

Blackout.

Silence.

The sound of an IED explosion. In its wake military radio chatter, the thudding of a helicopter, loud at first, then fading down.

CHARLIE *(voice over)* Your hearing's the last to go.

The radio crackle melds into the sound of a hospital, the digital heartbeat of medical machines, getting louder.

(voice over) And the first to come back.

The lights come up on a cloud of dust, still clearing from the stage. A hospital bed surrounded by screens, backlit. The silhouette of a man lying in the bed.

A **NON-CAUCASIAN NURSE** *enters and walks behind the screens. She carries a tray with a water bottle and a glass. She, too, is silhouetted as she works. As she dresses her patient's stump, he begins to stir.*

NURSE What's your name?

He stares at her, his breathing becoming rapid.

CHARLIE Fuck. You.

NURSE You're in Birmingham, in hospital—

CHARLIE /Fuck you, you Taliban bitch!/

NURSE Can you remember your name?

CHARLIE *(shouting)* Help! Help! I'm in here! Here!

He tries to get out of bed but fails.

NURSE You're in Selly Oak Hospital. Please, can you remember your name?

CHARLIE *(shouting)* A.N.A.! A.N.A.! A.N.A.!

NURSE You'll wake the other patients.

CHARLIE Help! Radio my position! Radio my position! A.N.A.! A.N.A.! A.N.A.!

NURSE Would you like some water?

CHARLIE A.N.A.! A.N. – ...Water?

She pours a glass of water.

Oh no you don't. You're going to poison me. You think I'm fucking stupid? You're going to kill me. That's fucking cleaning fluid!

NURSE It's from a bottle.

CHARLIE Show me.

She opens a fresh bottle in front of him and pours it into a plastic cup. As she approaches him, **CHARLIE** *knocks it from her hand.*

Fuck off! I'm a British soldier! Help! Over here! It was the terp, wasn't it? I bet it was the fucking terp.

He begins singing.

I'M 'ENERY THE EIGHTH, I AM,

*The **NURSE** exits. When she re-enters she is with a **BRITISH OFFICER** in British military uniform. Both enter the screens. **CHARLIE** stops singing.*

CHARLIE You fucking turncoat! You motherfucking traitor! I swear, when I get out of here I am going to rip out your throat, shit down your neck and wipe your fucking gene pool from the face of the earth.

*The **OFFICER** nods, then leaves.*

NURSE You're in Birmingham. In hospital. They'll move you off the ward if you carry on like this.

CHARLIE *(between bursts of song)* Yeah, Birmingham, of course I am. Birming – fucking – ham? I don't think so. Boss! Boss! Don't leave me in here! Don't leave me!

*The **OFFICER** enters. He is with a young woman, **LAUREN**. They both walk behind the screens.*

*At first **CHARLIE** doesn't see her. He continues his shouting and swearing.*

LAUREN Charlie? Charlie, it's me.

He turns to look at her and immediately starts crying.

CHARLIE Oh Jesus. Lauren, how did they get you? I swear, when I get out of here I am going to kill every motherfucking one of you. Baby, have they hurt you? Did they torture you? If you've touched one hair on her head—

LAUREN, *shocked, begins to leave. The **OFFICER** exits with her. He returns with an older woman, **CHARLIE'S MOTHER**.*

CHARLIE'S MOTHER Charles? It's your mother. Calm down now, calm down.

CHARLIE Mum? No, no, not you too. No, this has to stop! Stop stop stop stop!

The cubicle goes dark. **CHARLIE** *suddenly bursts through the downstage screen, falling to the ground. He is in uniform. He stands, one leg missing, and leans on his crutch. He looks at the audience.*

You know when you fell off your bike? As a kid? Do you remember that pain? The one you don't feel at first, but then you look down at your hand, your knee and it's all gritty from where you bounced along the pavement. And that's when it comes on, pulsing, and you're like, "Ow, ow, ow, what the fuck?"

That's what I remember. That kinda feeling. Grit in my hands, my knees.

In my mouth. The taste of it.

And the smell of Afghan. Gritty and shitty. Sand, skin flakes and shit.

That's what I remember.

Beat.

I don't remember waking up.

I don't remember eating breakfast.

I don't remember being given orders, or loading up, or leaving the compound.

I don't remember going where we went.

I don't remember walking through an archway, a low archway.

I don't remember the IED going off.

None of that.

Beat.

What I *do* remember is taking down our ponchos the night before because there was a heelo coming in the next day. Then lying down in my trench on some shitty deflated air mattress and looking up at the Afghan stars which, let me tell you, are like no other fucking stars anywhere else.

Next thing I know, I'm being tortured by the fucking Taliban. For three weeks.

If anyone tries to tell you an induced coma is any kind of fun, they're fucking lying. So, yeah, I realise I must have looked like a class A asshole back there just now, but you have to understand I wasn't *in* that hospital bed. Sure, I *was* in that bed, and as far as my fiancée and my mother were concerned I was there. Their Charlie was back. But at the same time he wasn't.

That round light above me? That was an observation hole. The screens? A temporary Taliban holding station. The nurse? Some devious fucking interrogator. The pain and the tubes? That was the torture.

"I'm 'Enry The Eighth, I Am?" No fucking idea. Didn't even know that song had more than two lines.

Beat.

When British soldiers were wounded in the Napoleonic Wars it took them months to get home, if they did. In World War One a fortnight at least. World War Two, about the same from France, much longer from India, Egypt, Burma.

Now? Medevaced from Nad Ali North to Bastion in twenty minutes, back in the UK in twelve, thirteen hours tops. But in here –

He taps his head.

Even quicker than that. Pretty much insta-fucking-taneous. Blink of an eye kinda stuff. With a few weeks high-definition hallucinations thrown in for free.

The only problem is that when you come back that quick not all of you comes back at once.

He lifts up his stump.

And I don't mean the fucking obvious either.

Beat.

There was this one time, on Herrick five. I was out on patrol. Sangin. Some kids came up. They were talking to one of the A.N.A. soldiers. I asked him what they wanted. He said, "They want to know where you are from?" I said, "Tell them the other side of the world." So he did. But then the terp started laughing. I asked him what was so funny. He said, "He told them you were from another world."

At the time I told the terp to correct him. But now, well, I kinda think he might have had it right the first time round.

Beat.

Before we get any further I can see more than one of you out there are thinking, "What kind of an accent is that for a *Royal* Marine anyway?" Well I'll tell you, my friends. Canadian, that's what, and don't you fucking forget it. Or the Fijians, the Trinidadians, the Gambians, the Gurkhas. Oh yeah, thanks to your over-industrious forebears we're all in this Afghan shit together, all us citizens of the Commonwealth.

And now, for the brief time *we* have together, so are you. So, shall we get started?

He throws a wide smile.

Let's go on a tour.

Scene Two – Histories

CHARLIE *stands to attention.*

CHARLIE PO56085M.

Corporal Charles Fowler.

Aged twenty eight.

B company twenty two commando, Royal Marines.

Injured in Nad Ali North, September 23rd 2011.

I was on a section assault on a compound when a western flank stepped on an IED. Op was successful. Casevaced from the area to Bastion and then to Selly Oak Hospital, UK. After three weeks in a medically induced coma, I spent four weeks at QE, then straight to Headley Court.

Halfway through his speech CHARLIE *is joined on stage by* LEROY, *who also begins reciting his history as* CHARLIE *continues his at a lower volume. This pattern is repeated with each soldier entering earlier and earlier in the previous soldier's speech until the stage is filled with wounded* SOLDIERS *reciting their histories.*

LEROY 25044898.

Rifleman Leroy Jenkins.

Aged twenty two.

Fourth batt The Rifles.

Injured on 26th July 2009, Helmand Province, Afghanistan.

Left leg blown off in an IED strike, medevaced back to the UK.

Recovery in Selly Oak Hospital, Birmingham, for eight weeks. Right leg amputated. Rehab at Headley Court for a year. Awaiting medical discharge at Tedworth House.

DANIEL 542711.

Major Daniel Thomas.

Aged thirty nine.

Second Battalion Royal Welsh.

Suffered a traumatic brain injury in an IED strike on 4th July 2009 whilst commanding a company in Babaji, Afghanistan.

Medevaced to Bastion, Kandahar, Queen Elizabeth Hospital, Birmingham.

Discharged after six weeks.

Spent seven months in Headley Court for brain rehabilitation.

Awaiting medical discharge.

JOHN 25223563.

Sapper John Booth.

Aged twenty.

Nine Parachute Squadron RE.

Injured on 19th July 2008, PB Armargh, Sangin, Helmand Province. Taliban ambush on a vector rescue op. IED blast to rear of Wimik – blown sixty feet into Taliban firing point. QRF on quadbike taken back to FOB Jackson, Sangin. Medevaced to Camp Bastion, then Queen Elizabeth and Selly Oak.

Broken back four places, broken leg, arm, shattered heel, shrapnel legs, thigh, groin, lung contusion, head injury, ten-week strict bed rest. Told would never walk again, wheelchair-bound, intensive rehab. After treatment returned to frontline September 2010, but forced to return after nine months due to previous injuries. Awaiting spinal surgery and rehabilitation.

FRANK PO63793G.

Corporal Frank Taylor.

Aged twenty five.

Special Forces Support Group.

Injured on 1st Feb 2007 in Helmand Province.

Hit by RPG blast as storming Taliban compound. Casevaced via Black Hawk to Kandahar for initial treatment. Once stabilised flew back to Selly Oak Hospital, Birmingham. After six weeks began recovering physically but mentally struggling. Currently seeing psychologists in an establishment in Berkshire.

ROGER 25886967.

Corporal Roger Smith.

Age thirty seven.

B Company.

Two PWRR.

Injured on 26th August 2008 in Nad Ali, Afghanistan. I was commanding a Snatch three hundred metres short of jab when the vehicle hit an IED. I was blown clear of the vehicle, landing on my right shoulder and neck. Medivaced to Bastion. I had prolapsed discs at C5–C7 in my upper spine and a dislocated shoulder. Casevaced back to UK. Sent to Selly Oak Hospital, Birmingham, where discs at C6 and C7 were replaced. Presently undergoing rehab at Headley Court.

JEAN W25031076.

Sergeant Jean Barker.

Aged twenty six.

Twenty six Engineer Regiment eight Squadron.

Injured on 15th June 2011. I was in a convoy in the lower Sangin valley when my Pinzgauer hit an IED. I was thrown from the vehicle, sustaining two broken ankles and a damaged lower back. Medevaced from blast area to Camp Bastion. Flown to UK to Selly Oak Hospital. Sent back to regiment with ongoing physio.

Awaiting below-knee amputation of right leg and reconstruction of left ankle. Also receiving treatment for PTSD. Discharge date, 11th April 2012.

DARREN 25051100.

Bombardier Daz Sobey.

Aged thirty four.

Twenty sixth Regiment Royal Artillery.

Injured on April 2007 on Salisbury Plain whilst commanding one hundred and five milimetre artillery light gun.

Gun crew accidently crushed me bringing gun into action. Spinal damage and losing use of left arm. Had spinal surgery but remain in chronic pain and reliant on strong medication.

Awaiting medical discharge.

CHRIS 24652173.

Colour Sergeant Chris Ward.

Aged forty three.

First Battalion Royal Green Jackets.

Injured in July 2006 by an IED while on patrol in Sangin valley. Lost both legs, two fingers and both bollocks. Eight weeks at Selly Oak hospital, then fourteen months at Headley Court before voluntary medical discharge. Mentor for the Not Forgotten Association.

ALI 25108692.

Sergeant Ali Briggs.

Aged thirty six.

First Battalion Royal Anglian Regiment.

Injured on 17th June 2007 on Herrick six when a mortar round landed in my forward operating base. Shrapnel in my legs, mainly right knee. Casevaced to Bastion where initially treated, then flown back to Selly Oak Hospital, Birmingham. Transferred to Headley Court for intensive rehab. Awaiting elective below-knee amputation.

SIMI W1042163.

>Lance Corporal Simi Yeats.

>Aged thirty eight.

>Injured 16 June 2010 in Hameln, Germany. Damage to left knee. Realignment of left leg at Frimley Park Hospital. Undergoing physio and rehabilitation at Headley Court, pending army career outcome.

DAVID 25014876.

>Captain David Phillips.

>Aged thrity seven.

>Nine Parachute Squadron Royal Engineers.

>Injured on Herrick eight, 2008 Sangin, Afganistan.

>Mortar attack. Suffered shrapnel wounds to the stomach and leg. Medevaced to Camp Bastion and transferred to Selly Oak Hospital, Birmingham.

>There for six weeks, three of them in an induced coma. Transferred to Headley Court. Remained for seven months. Suffer from PTSD.

Scene Three – Joining

The **SOLDIERS** *remain in their positions. They begin humming.* **CHARLIE** *takes a step forward.*

[MUSIC: "MEN OF HARLECH"]

CHARLIE I joined up for a bet. I saw an advert for the Royal Marines – "99.9% Need Not Apply". So I applied.

As each **SOLDIER** *speaks they also take a step / wheel forward.*

DANIEL I was working in Tesco when I read an article about Sandhurst being short of officers.

ROGER Well the Gulf War had kicked off, hadn't it? Everyone wanted a gun. *I* wanted a gun. My father-in-law had been giving me grief – telling me I couldn't handle it. So I joined. That fucking showed him.

DARREN Family tradition. My father was artillery, my uncle's artillery, my great-great-grandfather was artillery. Even my nan was an ack-ack gunner.

FRANK When I saw the Twin Towers go down, well, I thought I wanted to be part of it, you know, help sort it out. I was a bricklayer at the time but we'd had a hard couple of winters and we had our son on the way. So yeah, I joined for my family too.

LEROY I can't remember the Twin Towers. I was ten years old when that happened. In my family though, every male has to serve in the army. I joined as soon as I could, when I was sixteen. My mother wanted me to wait. She'd already lost two of my brothers. One in the Falklands, another in the Gulf.

CHRIS I wanted to be a copper, but my dad said coppers don't have no mates, so we went down the careers office and I joined the army instead. Royal Green Jackets. My old man was dead proud.

ALI His dad was right. Coppers don't have no mates. My grandfather said I'd never amount to anything. When he died I joined up. When I passed out and saw the look on my mum's face I thought great, two birds, one stone. I made my grandad proud and my mum don't think I'm a knobhead anymore.

JOHN I just always wanted to. Ever since my older brother gave me this tank you built yourself. I was always running round the woods, that kind of thing. I signed up when I was sixteen. My mum's always supported me. Always.

JEAN It was a way out to be honest. I had an attitude problem. Was either the army way or the other way, if you know what I mean. The police and my parents pushed me in.

DAVID Every man in my family's served. Crimean War, Boer War, World War One, World War Two. Do you know Psalm 144? It was written in the front of our family bible – "Blessed be the Lord, my strength, which teacheth my hands to war, and my fingers to fight." But it's about security too. For my family. Stability.

The **SOLDIERS** *remain in their final positions.*

Scene Four – Recruitment

[MUSIC: "HIS EYE IS ON THE SPARROW"]

Three women enter, Frank's girlfriend: **MICHELLE**, *John's mother:* **TRACY** *and Charlie's fiancée:* **LAUREN**.

MICHELLE He said he was doing it for all of us, our future. And I still believe him. He was. We had our Liam on the way and, well, we needed the money. So yeah, of course I supported him.

TRACY My husband, his stepdad, he was in the army. So, yeah, I know what it's like. What they're like. And I know he's always wanted to join, from when he was little.

LAUREN We met two weeks before he went for his basic training. I was working in a pub. He had to have three shots of tequila before he had the courage to ask me out. He was full of it, even then.

MICHELLE He really wanted to do something. He wanted to make a difference. And he did, I'm sure of it. There was just so much we didn't know, wasn't there? About what it was going to be like. When he went away. Afterwards.

TRACY But, at the end of the day he's my son, isn't he? He's my baby. I'd never stop him, but, well, it's hard, yeah, it is. Seeing your boy go off like that.

LAUREN I could see straight away there was no way he wouldn't go. And I was never going to ask him to choose, was I? I mean, who wants to hear they come second?

A single spotlight upstage discovers **SIMI**. *She begins walking downstage, singing..*

SIMI
>I SING BECAUSE I'M HAPPY
>I SING BECAUSE I'M FREE
>FOR HIS EYE IS ON THE SPARROW
>AND I KNOW HE WATCHES ME

The other women exit.

When I was seven I had a dream. I was going to live where the Queen lived. And I was going to be a soldier.

I'd seen her when she came to visit on Independence Day. All of us were lining the streets of San Fernando, waving. And she waved back. She had a pink hat, and a matching suit. And as she waved I was shouting, "I'm going to live where you live! I'm going to live where you live!"

And then I had my dream. I told my mother about it while she was combing my hair.

YOUNG SIMI *enters and kneels in front of* **SIMI***, who begins combing her hair.*

YOUNG SIMI There were four of us, four girls. My mother kept forgetting our names, so in the mornings when she was getting us ready for school, she numbered us instead, one to four. I was number three.

Beat.

Mummy?

SIMI *(as her mother)* Keep your head still, child!

YOUNG SIMI I had a dream last night.

SIMI *(as her mother)* You always dreaming some stupidness!

YOUNG SIMI No, Mum! This is a good one.

SIMI *(as her mother)* You always say it's a good one. Go on then. What is it?

YOUNG SIMI I dreamt I was a soldier and I lived where the Queen lives.

SIMI *(as her mother)* Where the Queen lives? Where the Queen lives? I told you it was a stupid dream! You know where the Queen lives?

YOUNG SIMI No.

Beat.

But I can find out.

SIMI *(as her mother)* Look, child, get to school before you're late! And stop talking your stupidness!

She ushers **YOUNG SIMI** *away.*

YOUNG SIMI *(to audience)* Joining the army wasn't even a thought in my family. I had no father, so Mum was both mum and dad. Every time I mentioned my dream she went ballistic.

SIMI Of course I did! You know what it is to have a girl-child in the Caribbean and be mother, father, everything? You have to keep them close. Where you can see them, reach them.

YOUNG SIMI If I was playing in the backyard and went out the gate, she'd come out to pull me back in.

SIMI You was too far for me to reach out that gate. Too far.

YOUNG SIMI But I wanted to do something different. I wanted to go to England. I wanted to be a soldier. So one day I woke up and I told her. I was going.

The two women look at each other

SIMI Too far. Too far.

YOUNG SIMI *walks upstage towards a recruiting office.*

YOUNG SIMI Two weeks after I got to England I saw an advert. "Be the Best", it said. "Join the British Army." I got on a bus to Edgware, came out of the station and there, in front of me, was a careers centre. So I walked in.

She enters the recruiting office where **CHRIS** *sits behind a desk.*

CHRIS Afternoon, how can I help you?

YOUNG SIMI I'd like to join the army.

CHRIS Well, you've come to the right place. Are you local?

YOUNG SIMI No. I'm from Trinidad. San Fernando. I have my passport.

CHRIS Right, fair enough. Well, let's get started, shall we? How old are you?

As **CHRIS** *asks the question the lights come up on another recruiting office upstage.* **JOHN** *and his mother,* **TRACY**, *sit across a desk from* **ROGER**.

JOHN Sixteen.

TRACY Two months ago. August.

ROGER Right, thanks. And was it always the Paras that interested you, John?

JOHN Yeah.

ROGER And why's that?

JOHN Well, they're the best, 'ent they?

ROGER We like to think so. Enjoy your outdoor stuff? Skydiving, water skiing in Cyprus, scuba diving – *(to* **TRACY***)* there's some brochures there if you want to take a look – muff diving.

TRACY How long is the training again?

As she asks this, the lights come up on another office downstage. **DANIEL** *sits across a desk from* **FRANK**.

DANIEL Thirty-two weeks, if you pass everything first time.

FRANK My girlfriend's pregnant. Will I be away for all that time?

DANIEL No. There's a break halfway though. Any marriage plans?

FRANK We thought we'd wait until I'd finished training.

DANIEL Right. Well, yes, that could work. If you pass out on a Friday, you'll be reporting for duty with your new unit on the Monday morning. So there's a couple of days there.

FRANK It's that quick?

As he asks the question the lights come up on another office downstage. LEROY *sits across a desk from* CHARLIE, *who wears his prosthetic leg.*

LEROY Can be. A year from now you could be in Afghan. Norway. Belize.

CHARLIE Sweet.

LEROY And that stuff you hear about women and the uniform? All fucking true. You get your green beret, women all over your cock.

CHARLIE So when can I get started?

LEROY You can start now if you want to mate. I'll just get the forms and we'll get cracking.

He wheels away from the desk, revealing he has no legs. As he returns to the desk.

Everything alright, mate?

CHARLIE Yeah, sorry. It's just. I didn't realise… um, well, you've got no legs.

LEROY Well, at least you'll pass the observation test.

Beat.

Look, you're making the right choice, Charlie. When you join the corps you join a family. You'll make friends who'll be closer to you than brothers.

Yeah, shit happens, but I wouldn't change any of it. I lost my legs, but I saved my best friend's life that day. You any idea what that feels like? To care *that* much about something, to care *that* much about doing your job?

CHARLIE No.

LEROY Sign here today and you will.

All four recruits, **YOUNG SIMI, JOHN, FRANK** *and* **CHARLIE** *sign simultaneously.*

YOUNG SIMI *turns towards the audience.*

YOUNG SIMI I signed up for twenty-two years. Then I got on the bus and went back to my aunty's. When I came in the door I told her, "Aunty, I'm a soldier." I was living my dream.

The other recruits also face the audience. They all raise one hand. **YOUNG SIMI** *begins the Oath of Allegiance. The others join her in turn until they are all reciting the oath.*

I swear by Almighty God that I will be faithful and bear true allegiance to Her Majesty Queen Elizabeth II, her heirs and successors—

CHARLIE —and that I will as in duty bound, honestly and faithfully defend Her Majesty, her heirs and successors—

JOHN —in person, crown and dignity against all enemies—

FRANK —and will observe and obey all orders of Her Majesty, her heirs and successors—

ALL —and of the generals and officers set over me. So help me God.

Scene Five – Training

As the recruits come to the end of the oath they are joined by **JOHN** *and* **DAVE**. *The sound of a train leaving a station. They loiter. Some light cigarettes.*

Suddenly **DARREN** *marches through them, screaming orders.*

DARREN Oi! You lot, get fell in! That means get into a fucking line!

Put out that fag, you scraggy little shit! You! Stand up straight! Don't you fucking look at me like that, you fucking fuck! Get that fucking hoodie down! You're in a new gang now! You two, Pinky and Perky, put those fucking phones away!

JOHN Sorry, sarge.

DARREN Sarge? Sarge? Would you like me to massage your passahge with my sausahge? I'm a bombardier, shitlips!

He turns on the audience.

What you fucking looking at? You! Get a haircut. You! Sit up straight. Don't you fucking smile at me, sonny boy! You think I'm funny, do you? Well, we'll soon see about that.

As **DARREN** *marches the recruits around the stage, the music begins.*

[MUSIC: "TRAINING SONG"]

YOU WILL NOT CALL ME "MATE",
I AM NOT YOUR FRIEND.
YOU WILL NOT CALL ME "SIR",
I AM NOT YOUR FRIEND,
YOU WILL CALL ME "BOMBARDIER",
YOU WILL LOOK AT ME WITH FEAR,
FOR NO MATTER HOW SWEET I MAY APPEAR,
I AM NOT YOUR FRIEND!

    WHEN I SAY "SIT UP", YOU DO. YES, WE DO!
    WHEN I SAY "BRACE UP", YOU DO. YES, WE DO!
    WHEN I SAY "STAND TO", STAND TO. YES, WE DO!
    YOU WILL NEVER ASK ME WHY.
    AND WHEN I SAY "JUMP!",
    YOU WILL ASK

DARREN & SOLDIERS
    "HOW HIGH?"

DARREN
    POLISH BOOTS IS WHAT YOU DO. YES, WE DO!
    YOU LOVE STARCH AND BRASSO TOO. YES, WE DO!
    THINKING YOU CAN LEAVE TO ME.
    UNIFORM IS YOUR I.D.
    IN YOUR SLEEP, YOU'LL DREAM PT. YES, WE DO!

    JUST ONE WAY TO SURVIVE;
    YOU ALL WORK AS A TEAM.
    TO MAKE IT OUT ALIVE,
    YOU ALL WORK AS A TEAM.
    CLOSE AS TWINS INSIDE THE WOMB,
    CLOSE AS CORPSES IN A TOMB,
    LIKE A BRIDE ASTRIDE A GROOM,
    YOU ALL WORK AS A TEAM.

    FEEL THE BURN, ENJOY THE PAIN. FEEL THE BURN!
    PAIN IS PLEASURE, TELL YOUR BRAIN. FEEL THE BURN!
    YOU'RE ALIVE, SO PAIN IS GAIN! FEEL THE BURN!
    FEELING PAIN YOU WON'T SUCCUMB,
    AND YOU WON'T FEEL FEAR TILL YOU'RE FEELING NUMB.

    CLEAN YOUR RIFLE, THEN YOURSELF.

SOLDIERS
    MY WEAPON, MYSELF!

DARREN
    THINK OF RIFLE, THEN YOURSELF.

SOLDIERS
>MY WEAPON, MYSELF!

DARREN
>WHEN YOUR RIFLE'S REALLY CLEAN,
>AND BY CLEAN I MEAN PRISTINE,
>YOU CAN LOAD YOUR MAGAZINE.

SOLDIERS
>MY WEAPON, MYSELF, MY WEAPON, MYSELF, MY WEAPON, MYSELF, MY WEAPON, MYSELF, MY WEAPON, MYSELF, MY WEAPON, MYSELF, MY WEAPON, MYSELF!

DARREN *(spoken)* Squad will move to the right in file, right turn!

By fronts, quick march! Left right left right…

The recruits are marched off stage.

Scene Six – Briefing 1

DANIEL *enters with a white screen. A map of Afghanistan is projected onto it. He addresses the audience as if at a military briefing.*

DANIEL Thank you, Sergeant Barker.

British forces first entered Afghanistan in 1839. This first Afghan War resulted in a British withdrawal.

The Second Afghan War was fought in 1878, again resulting in a British withdrawal.

We entered Afghanistan for a third time in 1919 and withdrew the same year, celebrated annually on Afghan Independence Day on 19th August.

These three Afghan wars are sometimes referred to as "The Great Game".

A communist-backed coup precipitated an invasion by the Soviet Union in 1979. This invasion was resisted by the Mujahidin, resulting in Soviet withdrawal ten years later in '89.

Between '92 and 2001 the Taliban gained control of the country. They imposed strict Sharia law and provided a safe haven for Al-Qaeda.

The Taliban were overthrown by the Northern Alliance and US/UK forces in 2001. They still remain active in southern parts of the country including Helmand Province, where British forces have had locations in Sangin, Kajaki, Musa Qala, Nad Ali, Gereshk, Lashkar Gah, Garmsir and many more.

Helmand Province covers a total area of fifty-nine thousand square kilometres, larger than Wales and Northern Ireland put together. In 2002 the British had three hundred troops on the ground. In 2005 we had three thousand, in 2012, nine thousand five hundred. We currently have around six thousand servicemen and women in the country.

Afghanistan has always been a strategic crossroads for the region, and in today's operating environment its neighbours Pakistan and Iran both have significant interests in the country. Some of the players have changed, but the playing field remains the same.

The Great Game, ladies and gentleman, continues.

DANIEL *exits.*

Scene Seven – Field Medic Course

The call to evening prayer from a minaret. A song in the style of Snow Patrol's **["CHASING CARS"]** *plays faintly in the background*.

DAVID *and* **ROGER** *march in with* **JOHN**, *who wears full combat uniform, osprey, helmet.* **DAVE** *carries a litre bottle of water. The three of them enter a tight spotlight far downstage. When they speak they all address the audience directly.*

DAVID Right, forget what you learnt on your FA1s, BCTD, CFX or whatever. For the next six months this is the only course you need to remember. If you listen up it'll either save your life or one of your oppos, so listen up good. John!

Now, John here 'as kindly agreed to be our puppet today. Say hello, John.

JOHN Hello, John.

DAVID As you can see, John's all kitted out to take on the Tali. Helmet, osprey, weapon system. Combined weight of seventy to eighty kg. It's hot today, isn't it? Well, get used to it, because it's always fucking hot. Except when it's cold, and then it's fucking cold. Either way, whatever the weather, you're going to be spending a lot of your time out here carrying this load.

ROGER *points to a member of the audience.*

ROGER Want to know what that feels like?

---

* A licence to produce THE TWO WORLDS OF CHARLIE F does not include a performance licence for "CHASING CARS". The publisher and author suggest that the licensee contact PRS to ascertain the music publisher and contact such music publisher to license or acquire permission for performance of the song. If a licence or permission is unattainable for "CHASING CARS", the licensee may not use the song in THE TWO WORLDS OF CHARLIE F but should create an original composition in a similar style or use a similar song in the public domain. For further information, please see Music Use Note on page iii.

He points at another person in the audience.

Like having him on your back. All day. But however tired you might get, you do *not* reduce your kit. Why? Because everything you need to protect yourself, to survive or to save your mucka, is carried here, on your person.

ROGER *begins going through* **JOHN***'s pouches and pockets, pulling out the kit.*

Ammunition, bayonet, pistol, P.R.R., morphine – lose that and you *will* be in a world of pain! Field dressings, compression bandages. Celox gauze – remember every hole's a goal! Ashman's seal for those sucking chest wounds. Tourniquet! High and tight! Tight is right! And always check the back of the fucking wound too!

DAVID So much for the kit. Now let's get to the stuff that really matters.

(to **JOHN***)* Strip down, John.

JOHN *hesitates.*

ROGER You heard him. Down to your blast pants.

As **JOHN** *removes his uniform.*

DAVID Kit changes. Always has, always will. But human anatomy doesn't change. And that's why you'd better listen up good because this could make the difference between your mate going home on a stretcher or in a body bag.

He takes out a red marker pen. As he talks he draws on **JOHN***'s body.*

Let's start with the basics, shall we?

He holds up the bottle of water.

This is a litre of water. John's got five litres of blood in his body. He can lose a litre of that, no problem. Two litres, getting tricky. More than that, he should start to worry.

His heart, about the size of a fist, is here. When he starts oozing, *this* is pumping the juice through his arteries. Going south through his thoracic aorta, out here, along his arms, and down here, along his thighs. And up here, supplying his tiny mind, his carotid artery.

Right, so things have gone wrong for John and he's stepped on an IED. What injuries is he likely to sustain? Probably lose a leg, if he's lucky amputated here, or unlucky, here. So that's gone off in someone else's compound. What else? He'll be fragged here on his face, and here along the side of his neck. It's a conical blast wave, remember, so here under his arms too. Some big chunks out of his legs from the stones and crap on the ground.

Probably a chunk out of the arm, here. Fragged along side of the chest.

Where's his weapon gone? That's right, straight up into his grid. Broken jaw, fractured zygoma, bit of blast ear. Pressure injury to the lungs. Probably lose a few fingers too. What else are we forgetting? What's here, biggest bone in the body? That's right, his femur. Where's that going? Smash, into his pelvis. Serious injury? You bet! Dislocated shoulder. If he isn't wearing his shades, sand, dirt and stones in his eyes.

He points to **JOHN**'s *genitals.*

What's going to happen to this bad boy? If he's wearing his blast pants, hopefully nothing. If he's not?

The eyelets from his boots are going to fly up, penetrate his nut sack, sever his penis. It's one of the first questions they'll ask you. "Have I got my cock and balls?" If he's not wearing blast pants, you can tell him yes, but he'll be pissing in six different directions for the rest of his life. Probably lost both arse cheeks too. So, respect the men whose injuries we've learnt from, and wear those fucking pants!

Right, that's enough of you, John.

JOHN *takes a white towel and walks downstage, cleaning the marker pen from his body, turning the towel red.*

ROGER Bullet wounds! You're out on patrol and the tree line's opened up on you, like it does. Your mate's gone down, small entry wound on the front, big exit wound in the back. You've got to pack that exit wound while still laying down rounds in the opposite direction. So what you going to do?

ROGER's voice fades away as the spot tightens to isolate JOHN.

JOHN He's right, you know. Some things don't change. Weapons change. Battlefields change. Wars change. But there's one thing that's never changed.

He pats his own chest.

This. Fight with stones. Fight with swords. Fight with missiles. This is where the fight happens. This is where the speeches end. The resolutions. This is where victory or defeat happens. The politics. This is where war happens. Here. On the bodies of men. Boys. We try and take theirs apart. They try and take ours apart. It's as simple as that.

He turns and walks upstage. The lights come up to reveal a FOB – temporary showers and toilets, sandbags, Hesco blocks. The heads of ALI and ROGER can be seen above a screen in front of the toilets. ALI ducks below the screen. The sound of him vomiting. He reappears.

Scene Eight – Comms

DARREN *enters with a sack of mail.*

DARREN Mail's here, lads.

ALI Ah, at last! About fucking time too!

*Other **SOLDIERS** begin to gather around **DARREN** as he hands out the mail. **CHARLIE** and **CHRIS** wear their prosthetics so appear to have their legs intact.*

DARREN Ward... Smith... Phillips... Briggs...

ALI Get mine for me, will you, mate?

DARREN Taylor... Sir... Barker...

*As each **SOLDIER** receives their bluie or package they drift to a more private place.*

Barker... Barker...and Barker.

***JEAN** is given a pile of packages.*

CHARLIE You're crated, Barker. So crated.

DARREN Yeats... Booth... Fowler...

*As the **SOLDIERS** open their bluies, the letter writers appear.*

LAUREN Charlie, I miss you so much —

MICHELLE Hey, Babe! I hope you get this soon... never soon enough though, is it?

TRACY Dear son, a few more parcels for you. No chocolate this time, like you asked. But lots of Haribo and shower gel!

*The **SOLDIERS** continue to read their bluies as the female letter writers sing.*

[MUSIC: "LETTERS"]

LETTER WRITERS (*sung*)
> HOPE YOU GET THIS, HOPE YOU'RE SAFE, HOPE EVERYTHING'S ALRIGHT. MISS YOU.
> EVERYONE HERE IS THINKING OF YOU, WE'VE HEARD NOTHING ON THE NEWS. MISS YOU.
> LOOK AFTER YOURSELF, MY LOVE, AND COME HOME SOON.

CHRIS When you're in the FOBs most of the time bluies is all you get. Only once, maybe twice every two months. There's one I'll always remember. My daughter drew me a birthday cake. And my son, he's got special needs, see, but he managed to write his name. It might not sound like much, but I was crying. It chokes you up, it does.

JOHN You have to take yourself away, somewhere quiet. It makes you miss home, miss everyone there. You realise how long it'll be before you see them again.

SIMI For three months I didn't get any bluies. It took so long from Trinidad to England to Iraq. Every time the mail came, I'd just be waiting, feeling alone. The boys on camp even started writing to me, just so I'd have some mail! But then one day I saw a Trinidad and Tobago stamp. I couldn't believe it. I almost screamed down the whole of the R.H.Q. Seeing their names, Mummy's handwriting. I rubbed it all over my face, so it would stay with me. I even slept with it! Every time I turned over, I'd reach under my pillow to check it was there. Because it was a lifeline, that bluie. It really was. A lifeline home.

The **SOLDIERS** *begin to write. As their recipients open their letters the* **SOLDIERS** *sing.*

SOLDIERS (*sung*)
> PLEASE DON'T WORRY, I'M WITH A GOOD BUNCH OF LADS.
>   AND, YOU KNOW, WE LOOK OUT FOR EACH OTHER.
> SEND MY LOVE TO MUM AND DAD. I DON'T KNOW WHEN I'LL CALL AGAIN.
> ALL MY LOVE, ALL MY LOVE.

TRACY I saw Mr Roberts yesterday. Your old Geography teacher? He said everyone at school is so proud of you.

LEROY Alright, Big Rog! Bet you weren't expecting this. Send my best to the lads and let them know I'm doing fine – there are more nurses here at the Q.E. than I know what to do with!

MICHELLE P.S. Sent you a special treat – just so you don't forget what's waiting for you back home! But keep this one to yourself!

ROGER Leroy mate! All the lads say you're a jack bastard for pissing off early. Jonesy reckons you knew it was there but stepped on it anyway so you could dodge the rest of the tour. Mind you, can't blame you – those Q.E. nurses sound worth it!

FRANK You mustn't worry about me, baby, I'll be fine. But I am missing you loads. I think my balls are going to explode!

LEROY Hearing from the lads after I got back helped loads. Yeah, those bluies meant a lot.

LAUREN He asked me to send him porn, which I did. But I never sent him photos of *me* like that. I've seen too many of the ones sent by the other girls to fall for that. I mean, I'm not going to provide relief for the whole unit!

CHRIS I'm losing lots of weight in this heat. You'll have a new man when I come home!

CHARLIE I head out on a "camping trip" with the "boy scouts" next week. I'll call as soon as I can, I promise!

SOLDIERS *(sung)*	**LETTER WRITERS** *(sung)*
PLEASE DON'T WORRY, I'M WITH A GOOD BUNCH OF LADS. AND, YOU KNOW, WE LOOK OUT FOR EACH OTHER.	HOPE YOU GET THIS, HOPE YOU'RE SAFE, HOPE EVERYTHING'S ALRIGHT. MISS YOU.

> SEND MY LOVE TO MUM AND DAD. I DON'T KNOW WHEN I'LL CALL AGAIN.
>
> ALL MY LOVE, ALL MY LOVE.

> EVERYONE HERE IS THINKING OF YOU. WE'VE HEARD NOTHING ON THE NEWS. MISS YOU.
>
> LOOK AFTER YOURSELF, MY LOVE. AND COME HOME SOON.

DANIEL No one gets to keep their mobile phone. They're too easy to intercept. Or if the enemy get hold of the sim card, then they phone the families at home, tell them their son or daughter has been captured. Which isn't good. So each week we get twenty welfare minutes on the sat phone instead. It's great, to hear your wife's voice, to speak to the kids. But it's really hard too. You *feel* the distance. After speaking with them I have to try really hard to disconnect from them again. And saying goodbye, that's the hardest. Saying goodbye.

LETTER WRITERS *(sung)*
> KISS, KISS. LOVE YOU. KISS, KISS. LOVE YOU. P.S. P.S. LOVE YOU. LOVE YOU.

SOLDIERS *(sung)*
> ALL MY LOVE. ALL MY LOVE. ALL MY LOVE.

LETTER WRITERS *(sung)*
> KISS, KISS. LOVE YOU. KISS, KISS. LOVE YOU.

The singing repeats and fades as both groups return to reading their letters on either side of the stage.

ROGER *is watching* **JOHN**, *who looks distressed.*

ROGER Of course sometimes the news from home is bad news. There's always a few Dear Johns. But you can't have one of your boys out on patrol who hasn't got his head on the job. So you've got to sort them out, whatever it takes.

CHRIS Oi, Booth. What you got there?

FRANK She hasn't, has she? The bitch.

JOHN Yeah, she has.

CHRIS Come on then.

> CHRIS *takes the letter from* JOHN.

"Dear John" – Fuck, I can't believe she actually gets to write that. "Dear John, I know this will be hard for you to read, but please believe me this is even harder for me to say."

DARREN Yeah, I bet it is love, 'cos you've got mortars coming in and only ration packs for the next five months too, haven't you?

CHRIS "I'm just not sure I can do this anymore."

ALI More like she's doing some other bloke down the pub.

CHRIS "When I read about that soldier killed last week, I felt so sick, thinking it could have been you."

FRANK So you thought you'd bin him. Yeah, nice.

CHRIS "I know I said I would wait for you, but I didn't know it would be like this."

> CHRIS *hands the bluie back to* JOHN. *The* SOLDIERS *start singing A song in the style of Billy Ray Cyrus'* **["ACHY BREAKY HEART"]***.

> JOHN *cracks a smile.* ALL *exit except for* ROGER.

ROGER You've got to defuse stuff quickly, and humour's the best way to do that. Attack, like they say, it's the best form of defence, isn't it?

---

* A licence to produce THE TWO WORLDS OF CHARLIE F. does not include a performance licence for "ACHY BREAKY HEART". The publisher and author suggest that the licensee contact PRS to ascertain the music publisher and contact such music publisher to license or acquire permission for performance of the song. If a licence or permission is unattainable for "ACHY BREAKY HEART", the licensee may not use the song in THE TWO WORLDS OF CHARLIE F. but should create an original composition in a similar style or use a similar song in the public domain. For further information, please see Music Use Note on page iii.

Lights come up on **SARAH**, **DANIEL**'s *wife. She is dressed in funeral black, her head bowed.*

CHAPLAIN (*voiceover*) We are gathered here today to honour the life and memory of Lance Corporal Andrew Jones, a young man of extraordinary courage who was willing to lay down his life for the lives of others and to pay the ultimate sacrifice in the defence of his country.

Offstage, the **SOLDIERS** *begin singing* **["ABIDE WITH ME"]**. *The hymn continues under the following action.*

SARAH *walks downstage.*

SARAH It's wonderful when he calls, of course it is. What wife doesn't want to hear from their husband? To know he's safe... But it's so frustrating too.

I have to talk to him about all this ordinary stuff, when all I really want to ask him is were you shot at today? Are you OK? Are you going out on any more ops? But I can't, can I? Because he can't tell me. Because all I'll get is silence. And I understand that, I do. Because sometimes there are things I can't tell him either.

A phone rings. **SARAH** *answers. The lights come up on the other side of the stage to reveal* **DANIEL** *on a sat phone.* **FRANK** *waits a little way behind him.*

DANIEL Darling? Darling, it's me.

SARAH Oh, it's so good to hear you. How are you?

DANIEL I'm fine, fine.

SARAH Did you get the recipes?

DANIEL Yes, I did. Thanks. Though not sure I'm really doing them justice.

Beat.

SARAH How is it out there?

DANIEL Hot. Even hotter than before, if that's possible.

SARAH Right.

DANIEL And there?

SARAH All fine. Good. Been raining today. Lucy's at netball though, so...

DANIEL Oh yes. Yes, that's Tuesdays and Thursday's now, isn't it?

SARAH Yes. She sent you a bluie yesterday.

DANIEL Great. Did she get mine?

SARAH Not yet, no.

Beat.

DANIEL Did you hear about Jones?

SARAH Yes, I did. His poor mother. I've written to her.

DANIEL Yes, so have I.

Beat.

But you mustn't worry. Everything's fine, really.

SARAH Right. Yes.

The phone starts beeping.

DANIEL Look, darling, I think I'm about to run out of minutes. I'm so sorry. I'll top up tomorrow.

SARAH OK. Don't forget we'll be at your mother's next week.

DANIEL Yes. Of course. I love you.

SARAH I love you too.

The line goes dead. They both look at their handsets for a moment. **DANIEL** *hands the sat phone to* **FRANK**. *As* **FRANK** *dials,* **DANIEL** *walks downstage. Just before he speaks we see* **MICHELLE** *take* **SARAH**'s *place to answer* **FRANK**'s *call. She carries a baby with one hand, holds the phone in her other. We don't hear their conversation.*

DANIEL Sometimes I think we say more with our silences than we do with our words. But it has to be that way. And not just for security. If she knew what I was doing, well, it would be hell for her. But I understand it must be just as difficult not knowing. But what can we do? It's still worth it – hearing her voice. Speaking to Lucy. It's about staying in touch, isn't it? About staying in contact.

As soon as **DANIEL** *says the word "contact"—*

ALL SOLDIERS *(shouted)* CONTACT!

The sound of small arms fire, mortars, UGLs and RPGs.

The **SOLDIERS** *scramble for helmets and weapons and begin laying down rounds in a defensive shoot.*

FRANK *tries to turn off the sat phone, but fails.* **MICHELLE** *is left listening to the contact. She shout's* **FRANK***'s name into the phone but her voice is drowned by the gunfire.*

The sound of battle stops and a single spot lights **MICHELLE.**

MICHELLE I had to listen to that contact for over five minutes. Explosions. Bullets. Shouting. It was two weeks before I heard from him again.

Fade to black.

Scene Nine – Contact

CHARLIE *sits opposite a* **PSYCHOLOGIST**. *As they talk the silhouette of a Vallon man occasionally passes them.*

CHARLIE What's it like? Jeez, well, kinda like everything you imagine. And not. I mean, when I first got out there it was like I was watching *Apocalypse Now*. I didn't know where to look, where to go, what was dangerous, what was safe. You come off the Chinook and the heat hits you like a punch in the face. And the smell. Shit and dust. It was the first time I'd heard a proper weapons system, outside the firing range. And, I mean, it's being discharged *at* you. Crack/Thump. Crack/Thump. The crack of the bullet snapping the air, *then* the thump of the weapon.

PSYCHOLOGIST And what about your first contact? How did you find that?

CHARLIE Well, it kinda found us really. They attacked our compound and, I won't lie, doc, it was fucking great. It was like, finally, we get to do our job. We'd had weeks of just gash sweeps, sanger duty, that kinda shit. So to finally have a defensive shoot – it was the best day of my military career. It was simple, you know? They brought the fight to us. We won, they lost. We suffered no casualties, but lots of our guys got confirmed kills. So yeah, it felt really, really good.

The following speeches are projected onto the stage.

ROGER You can't tell how you'll react. When that first RPG went across our bonnet me and Jimmy just looked at each other then started laughing. A month later he was dead, killed by one.

FRANK Your training kicks in. There's so much adrenalin the body takes over. And you've got rounds coming the other way too, at you, so yeah, I was just trying to stay alive.

SIMI It was the kids that were my deepest surprise. On Telic Eight. Coming at you with automatic weapons, petrol bombs.

Eleven, twelve years old. And you have to make that choice. It's you or them. You fire some rounds over their heads, and you hope they run away. But if they don't then…

JOHN I loved my first contact. I was in an orchard with my mate Parry. A sniper's round just missed my head. I felt it brush past my face. We didn't have our gats, so we ran for it, back to the camp, with the whole orchard being thrown up around us. And Parry, he starts singing from behind me, "run rabbit run rabbit, run, run, run." Just over and over.

ROGER, FRANK and **JOHN** *enter as a patrol in full combat gear. They move very slowly in formation downstage.* **DANIEL***'s speech is also projected.*

DANIEL On patrol you've got your eyes down all the time, trying to follow the Vallon man's route exactly. Then the next day we'd be at a shura, a gathering of the local elders. And for all I knew the hand I was shaking had planted the bomb that blew up one of my boys the week before.

PSYCHOLOGIST And how did that experience change for you? Over the tours?

CHARLIE Well the war changed, didn't it? Afghanistan changed. I mean, on Herrick five it was Wild West stuff, bandit country. Ten-dollar Taliban doing Beirut unloads. A lot of spray and pray, shoot and scoot. But by Herrick fourteen it was proper guerrilla warfare. I mean Sangin was I.E.D. central. Low metal content, infrared switches, strapping bombs to donkeys. They were even planting decoys so they could watch how we examined them. You had to respect your enemy. I mean, the guy who did this to me did a really, really good job. It was a legacy I.E.D., laid a while ago. But the batteries – those batteries had been changed regularly, to keep it active.

PSYCHOLOGIST Were you out on patrol often?

CHARLIE Yeah. I mean, you've got to take the fight to them, haven't you? You can't just sit back in the compound with your thumb firmly up your ass. But I'll tell you, doc, that first time I stepped outside the gate, my mouth went dry. I had to take a sip from my CamelBak straight away because... well, we were suddenly outside our comfort zone. You *know* that once you're out that gate anything could happen, at any time. And that it probably will. Every day we were playing Afghan roulette.

ROGER We'd snake, spread out, change our routes. We had two Vallon men on most patrols, and E.C.Ms. But sometimes there was nothing you could do. There were some bad days. But there were good days too, you know, when you're seeing them drop.

FRANK We'd always be watching the atmospherics. If you see the women and children start to leave, or some bloke who might be dicking you, we'd go firm, straight away. Take no chances.

JOHN On my second tour we never saw them, not once. It was like fighting ghosts. When we did night ops sometimes they'd communicate by howling like animals, like dogs.

That could be pretty scary. I took a Pashtun language course before I went out. That helped loads. I could talk to people when we were out on patrol. Sometimes they'd tell us where the Taliban were, or warn us off certain routes.

PSYCHOLOGIST And what about relations with the locals? Did you have much interaction?

CHARLIE Well, yeah, sure, hearts and minds and all that. But that was the biggest change of all, doc. I mean, knowing *who* the enemy were. On the early tours you could bet anyone still in the smashed-up village you were occupying was up to no good. But then later? On Herrick twelve, thirteen, fourteen? It was a whole different ball game. Farmers, bazaars, kids, families. So the war card changed didn't it? You had to PID someone before you fired.

PSYCHOLOGIST PID?

CHARLIE Postively identify. Which I completely understand, but it was like we were stuck between these two fucking TLAs – PID and IED with old bootneck getting fucked over in the middle.

Beat.

The only way I can explain it is that you're not living with "if" anymore, but "when". A company loses a man and things change. The young ones want revenge. You're fighting for the man next to you. Fuck anything else. But at the same time you're waking up every day expecting something to happen. It's like there's five of you in a car, going on a road trip but you *know* at the end of that trip two of you will have lost your legs, one of you will be dead and another one will be wounded. You just don't know who, or when.

PSYCHOLOGIST Do you want to talk about your "when" Charlie?

Beat.

CHARLIE Sure. I was taking part in an op…

SIMI *enters. She begins singing her gospel song to the tune of* [**"HIS EYE IS ON THE SPARROW"**].

DANIEL I was commanding a company…

JOHN I was on top cover…

FRANK I was against a wall…

ROGER I was in a Snatch…

YOUNG SIMI I was in the comms room…

CHRIS I was on patrol…

ALL When/
   When/
   When/
   When…

A sudden simultaneous moment of contact. The sound of explosions and gunfire. In slow motion **FRANK** *is hit by an RPG.* **JOHN** *is blown from his vehicle.* **ROGER**'s *Snatch turns over.* **CHRIS, DANIEL, CHARLIE** *and* **LEROY** *are hit by IEDs.* **SIMI**, *still singing, has joined* **YOUNG SIMI** *in the centre of the stage.*

YOUNG SIMI There were two mortars, back to back. The first one killed my best friend. I was trying to get to him when the second one brought the wall down on me.

She kneels in front of **SIMI**.

I was trapped. They were trying to dig me out. But all I could hear was Mummy, singing the song we always sang.

As **YOUNG SIMI** *also starts singing* [**"HIS EYE IS ON THE SPARROW"**], **SIMI** *combs her hair, as in the earlier scene. All around them the moments of wounding continue.*

The **NON-WOUNDED SOLDIERS** *become medics. Shouts of "Man Down!" "Morphine", T1 casualty reports.*

JOHN *is crouched over* **CHRIS**. **DARREN** *over* **DANIEL**. *As the medics work the* **WOUNDED SOLDIERS** *sit up to speak.*

DANIEL I was blown twenty metres...

FRANK I heard the rocket coming in...

JOHN I was blown sixty feet...

CHRIS I caught the full force...

ROGER The Snatch went over and I hit the roof...

DANIEL The shrapnel went through the back of my brain...

FRANK It shattered my cheek bone, pierced my eye...

JOHN My mates thought I'd bought it, that I was pink mist...

CHRIS I tasted burnt flesh...

ROGER I could hear the others screaming, as it filled with water...

SIMI *and* **YOUNG SIMI**'s *singing fades to silence.*

JOHN And then there was silence...

FRANK Just this ringing in my ears, nothing else...

CHRIS Just a blue sky above me...

DANIEL And nothing else...

All lie down to be treated again. **LEROY** *sits up on the other side of the stage.*

LEROY My mate had been shot. So I was like, fuck this! Osprey off, helmet off, dropped my GPMG. Got him over my shoulder and ran for it. Then, everything went dark. No boom, no hitting the ground, no pain. I was just lying on the floor.

He lies back down as **JOHN** *and* **ROGER** *run over to him.*

JOHN Fuck! You alright, mate?

LEROY Yeah, yeah, I'm good.

ROGER Yeah, you fucking look it, mate.

LEROY What's that supposed to mean?

ROGER *and* **JOHN** *start treating him.*

JOHN You're going to be OK mate, you're going to be OK.

LEROY *looks up and sees his legs have gone.*

LEROY Fuck! Oh fuck!

ROGER You've been hit an IED. But you're going to be fine, you're going to be fine.

JOHN *checks his balls.*

JOHN You've still got your balls, mate.

LEROY Fuck, I'm going to die! I'm going to die! Give me a cigarette! Give me a cigarette!

ROGER You're not going to die.

JOHN We can't give you a fag, we can't, mate.

LEROY I'm going to fucking die, give me what I want!

> **JOHN** *hands him a fag, and lights it.* **JOHN**, **ROGER** *and* **LEROY** *all inhale deeply.*

I swear, that fag went down in one drag. My right leg was still hanging by a thread but as they carried me away it fell off and rolled into a ditch. I was like, "Get my leg, get my fucking leg." They couldn't reach it so the lads gave me a stick, said, "Here's your fucking leg." At the time I could have sworn it was. The last thing I remember is passing out in the chopper, thinking, "Fuck me, I didn't even have any last words." Apparently I came round again in Bastion. I was crying, screaming for my mum. But I don't remember any of that.

> *As* **ROGER**, **JOHN** *and* **LEROY** *exit.* **SARAH** *and* **LAUREN** *enter to stand in front of two screened hospital beds.*

SARAH For three weeks we experienced two different kinds of hell. He was suffering hallucinations in his coma, while I was out here, not knowing if he was going to live or die. It was strange, because he looked perfect. He was dirty, but he was tanned too, and really lean and fit. And his skin... they all come back with such good skin. Sand-blasted, smooth. But he wasn't perfect. Far from it.

Beat.

On the first night, just after he was brought in, I went to have a cup of tea in the waiting room. There were two other women in there, on their knees, on the floor, praying. They were wearing burkas. I know I shouldn't have, but I felt so angry at them. I mean Daniel was fighting for his life next door. But then I heard them say his name. Major Daniel

Thomas. And I realised they were praying for him. They were praying for all the patients on the ward.

LAUREN *paces up and down.*

LAUREN Please save him. Please, oh please. I promise if you do I'll come to church every week. I will. I'll go and see Mum more often. I'll cut back on the drink. I'll… I'll stop smoking. Really. I will. Just let him live. Please let him live.

A **NURSE** *enters.*

NURSE Miss Preston?

LAUREN Yes. That's me.

NURSE You're Charles's…

LAUREN Fiancée. Yes, yes, I am. Is he OK? Is he going to be alright?

NURSE Well, he's been really put through it. But yes. He's going to pull through.

She flings her arms around him.

LAUREN Oh God, thank you! Thank you so much! Can I see him?

NURSE Not yet. He's still in surgery. But in about an hour or so, that should be fine.

The **NURSE** *exits.* **LAUREN** *roots in her bag for a cigarette.*

LAUREN Oh thank you, thank you!

She pulls out a cigarette and is about to light it when she pauses. She looks up.

After this. OK? I promise. Last one.

The lights fade up on **CHARLIE** *and the* **PSYCHOLOGIST** *upstage.*

CHARLIE But like I said, I don't remember any of that. I was there, but I wasn't.

PSYCHOLOGIST Right.

The faint sound of military radio chatter, the thudding of a helicopter, building through his speech.

CHARLIE I don't remember waking up.

I don't remember eating breakfast.

I don't remember being given orders, or loading up, or leaving the compound.

I don't remember going where we went.

I don't remember walking through an archway, a low archway.

I don't remember the IED going off.

None of that.

Beat.

Just that taste. Grit in the mouth. And a few sounds, I guess. I remember a few sounds.

The sounds begin to fade.

But that's because it's the last to go, I guess. Your hearing. Your hearing's the last to go.

The sounds fade to silence.

Fade to black.

ACT TWO

Scene One – Physio

Physio Room.

Classical music plays*.

Lights come up to reveal an amputee wearing a regimental T-shirt sitting on a therapeutic ball working with his physiotherapist. Using a pair of bats they hit a bright orange balloon back and forth. Other patients enter, all wearing regimental T-shirts. Other physios also enter. They begin performing different exercises.

CHARLIE *enters on crutches.*

CHARLIE Welcome back. So, yeah, this is where we come afterwards. Personally I thought I was going to heaven. I'm not kidding, a lot of us here did. You're floating on the morphine, you're being casevaced into the heelo. There's this ringing in your ears and a blue sky above you. You've just been blown up – where do you think *you'd* be going?

Turns out I was wrong though. Wasn't heaven. It was Selly Oak. Then here.

Beat.

---

* A licence to produce THE TWO WORLDS OF CHARLIE F. does not include a performance licence for any third-party or copyrighted music. Licensees should create an original composition or use music in the public domain. For further information, please see Music Use Note on page iii.

It's a bit like doing basic training again – "break to build", that's what they told us back then. Well, we're sure as hell broken now, aren't we? So, plenty of building to be done. Learning drills and skills for our "new normal". Our new world. Our "brave new world". That has such creatures in it...

So yeah, this is, I guess, our new drill square. The physios our new P.T. instructors. The doctors, consultants, our majors and generals. Prosthetics, wheelchairs, meds, our new kit. The operations our, well, new operations. It's a bit of a freakshow to be honest with you. I wasn't too happy about it at first, I mean, a few weeks ago I was a steely-eyed dealer of death. Then, wham, bam, thank you mam, and I'm in this circus. Seals on bouncy balls. In Surrey.

He looks about the arches of the set.

And very nice it is too. Big grounds, gardens, orchards, regular Downton fucking Abbey.

As **CHARLIE** *takes his place in the physio room* **SIMI** *enters, wearing headphones. Her physio tells her to remove them.*

As she does the music switches from classical to dance.* The exercises begin to syncopate into a choreographed dance.

---

* A licence to produce THE TWO WORLDS OF CHARLIE F. does not include a performance licence for any third-party or copyrighted music. Licensees should create an original composition or use music in the public domain. For further information, please see Music Use Note on page iii.

Scene Two – Flashback

The physio dance routine is just starting to build when it is interrupted by a massive blast. A cloud of dust blows in from off stage. All the patients and physios collapse to the floor. The stage darkens. Torch beams sweep the scene as **TWO SOLDIERS** *in full combat gear,* **FRANK** *and* **DARREN**, *enter from the direction of the blast. They are panicked by what they see.*

DARREN Oh Jesus. Fuck, fuck! They're locals!

FRANK They said it was empty!

DARREN Well it obviously fucking wasn't, was it?

> **DARREN** *begins checking for signs of life.*

FRANK But we saw them leaving! We saw them fucking leaving!

> **DANIEL** *enters.*

DANIEL Jesus Christ! What the fuck is this, Sobey?

DARREN We didn't know, sir!

DANIEL Any survivors?

DARREN No, sir.

FRANK We saw them leave! We saw them fucking leaving!

DANIEL Zero Two Zero Alpha. Contact. Civilian casualties. Wait out. Move on through. Sobey? Clear?

> **DARREN** *moves to check their exit.*

DARREN Clear.

Taylor. For fuck's sake, Taylor!

> **FRANK** *and* **DARREN** *exit.* **DANIEL** *remains, looking at the bodies about him.*

DANIEL OPTAG prepares you for most things. But there's no training for this. Seeing it, smelling it. Which is why when some of us come back from Afghan, Afghan stays with us. Or us with it. You walk these corridors at night and believe me you'll hear a bit of Afghan behind every door. Sangin... Kajaki...

He begins to move upstage left, picking his way through the bodies.

Musa Qala... Nad Ali... Gereshk... Lashkar Gah... Garmsir... FOB Gibraltar... FOB Jackson... FOB Inkerman.

Scene Three – Sleep

DANIEL *exits. The bodies remain motionless for a moment before beginning to shift and turn. As the musical score gets louder they become syncopated, repeating a sequence of movements of discomfort.*

[MUSIC: " IT'S NOT RE-LIVING IT "]

WOMEN
IT'S NOT RE-LIVING IT. IT'S LIVING IT;
YOU'RE IN IT. YOU'RE THERE, DOING IT.

ALL
WORSE AT NIGHT, ALWAYS WORSE AT NIGHT.
WORSE AT NIGHT, ALWAYS WORSE AT NIGHT.

MEN
SCARED SCARED TO CLOSE MY EYES.
SCARED TO PUT MY HEAD ON THE PILLOW.

MEN	**ALL**
SCARED SCARED TO CLOSE MY EYES. SCARED TO PUT MY HEAD ON THE PILLOW.	IT'S NOT RE-LIVING IT; IT'S LIVING IT. YOU'RE IN IT. YOU'RE THERE, DOING IT.

ALL
WORSE AT NIGHT, ALWAYS WORSE AT NIGHT.
WORSE AT NIGHT, ALWAYS WORSE AT NIGHT.

JOHN For two years I couldn't sleep. Every fucking night. Just images, flicking through. Being blown up. Prodding through dead bodies in some fucking I.E.D. factory. Just all sorts of crazy shit, flicking, bouncing from one to the other. I'd be banging my head against the wall, just to take my mind of it then… then I'm like yeah, that fucking hurts.

DAVID *(solo)*
IT'S NOT RE-LIVING IT; IT'S LIVING IT.
YOU'RE IN IT. YOU'RE THERE, DOING IT.

ALL
>WORSE AT NIGHT, ALWAYS WORSE AT NIGHT.
>WORSE AT NIGHT, ALWAYS WORSE AT NIGHT

ROGER I had to stay up. I forced myself not to go to sleep. As soon as you close your eyes you see them again. All sorts of situations. Rounds going past your head. Bodies of kids floating downstream. And you think to yourself, "Why aren't I dead?"

SIMI
>SCARED, SCARED TO CLOSE MY EYES.
>SCARED TO PUT MY HEAD ON THE PILLOW.

WOMEN	**MEN**
IT'S NOT RE-LIVING IT; IT'S LIVING IT. YOU'RE IN IT, YOU'RE THERE, DOING IT.	SCARED, SCARED TO CLOSE MY EYES. SCARED TO PUT MY HEAD ON THE PILLOW.

LEROY Mine has its own timetable. It'll come and go. It's like, really awkward. It's space that brings it on. If I sleep in a double bed then I dream I'm on patrol again. But in my sleep I can control where we go. I still get blown up though. Every time. Sometimes I'm in my wheelchair, but no one says anything, like, "Why's Leroy in a fucking wheelchair?" But, yeah, if I sleep in a corner, up against a wall, holding my stumps, that makes it go away.

CHARLIE For my missus I'm the nightmare. Sweating, reaching for my weapon, taking cover across the carpet. She has to sleep in the corner of the bed. Or I just stay awake. Sometimes I hit myself in the face. To take my mind off it. Or you drink. Hopefully between finishing drinking and falling asleep you don't have too much time to think. Hopefully.

JOHN If you do you're fucked.

CHRIS Fucked.

ROGER Fucked.

ALL Fucked.

LAUREN He was drinking so much he'd just collapse into bed and then, God! The snoring! All night.

MICHELLE He thrashes around. And the sweating. The sweating's the worst. One night he was shouting, "Contact! Contact!" So I touched him, to wake him, and... and he punched me in the face.

SARAH For months he didn't sleep. He doesn't like the silence, it gives him time to think. I have it too. It was five in the morning when they came to tell me. And now I wake every morning at five. That knock on the door, it's in my head, in my body clock, forever.

WOMEN
IT'S NOT RE-LIVING IT; IT'S LIVING IT.
YOU'RE IN IT, YOU'RE THERE, DOING IT.

ALL
WORSE AT NIGHT, ALWAYS WORSE AT NIGHT.
WORSE AT NIGHT, ALWAYS WORSE AT NIGHT.

MEN
SCARED, SCARED TO CLOSE MY EYES.
SCARED TO PUT MY HEAD ON THE PILLOW.

MEN	**WOMEN**
SCARED, SCARED TO CLOSE MY EYES. SCARED TO PUT MY HEAD ON THE PILLOW	IT'S NOT RE-LIVING IT; IT'S LIVING IT. YOU'RE IN IT, YOU'RE THERE, DOING IT.

ALL
WORSE AT NIGHT, ALWAYS WORSE AT NIGHT.
WORSE AT NIGHT, ALWAYS WORSE AT NIGHT.

JOHN It's the pain that triggers it. It's always there, bubbling away, but worse at night. Always worse at night.

CHRIS Sometimes I just cry, because of the pain, the things it makes me think about.

LEROY It won't go away. It makes me want to smash something. I can't do anything to stop it. Like nails under the skin.

ROGER It's all down the left side of my neck, in my brain, down my shoulder and into my back. I try to put it in on a shelf, over there. I use distractions too – reading poetry, stripping my weapons, a shit load of drugs. But then sometimes it just takes over and that's when I have to ring the kids' mum and say, "I can't have them this weekend." And that's terrible, because it's my kids that keep me going.

All exit.

Scene Four – Briefing 2

DANIEL *enters upstage in his major's uniform. He begins to walk downstage.*

DANIEL Nostalgia

Melancholia

Wind

Contusions

Soldier's Heart

Abreaction

Effort Syndrome

NYDM (Not Yet Diagnosed – Mental)

NYDN (Not Yet Diagnosed – Nervous)

Exhaustion

Battle Exhaustion

Combat Exhaustion

Shell Shock

Neurasthenia

Traumatic Neurosis

Psycho Neurosis

Fear Neurosis

Battle Neurosis

Lack of Moral Fibre

Old Sergeant Syndrome

War Syndrome

Combat Fatigue

Acute Stress Disorder

Acute Stress Reaction

Combat Stress Reaction

Post-Combat Disorder
Post-War Disorder
Post-Traumatic Illness
Post-Traumatic Disorder
Post-Traumatic Stress Disorder

DANIEL *exits.*

Scene Five – Common Room

The common room of a P.R.U. A group of wounded and injured **SOLDIERS** *congregate around a* **SINGING TEACHER** *who leads them in* ["**THE GRAND OLD DUKE OF YORK**"].

ALL
THE GRAND OLD DUKE OF YORK,
HE HAD TEN THOUSAND MEN,
HE MARCHED THEM UP TO THE TOP OF THE HILL
AND HE MARCHED THEM DOWN AGAIN.
AND WHEN THEY WERE UP THEY WERE UP,
AND WHEN THEY WERE DOWN THEY WERE DOWN
AND WHEN THEY WERE ONLY HALFWAY UP,
THEY WERE NEITHER UP NOR DOWN.

SINGING TEACHER No, no, no. Stop, stop. Enunciate, Enunciate. The Grand Old Duke of York!

LEROY *(wheeling away)* This is bollocks.

SINGING TEACHER Leroy. Leroy, where are you going?

LEROY For a fag.

LEROY *exits.*

Others begin to drift away.

SINGING TEACHER Right, OK. Yes, OK, let's take a break. Fifteen minutes. Back here at two!

The **SOLDIERS** *disperse.* **CHRIS** *is on his laptop. The others sit in a group.*

ALI Who does he think we are? The Army wives choir?

FRANK Ah come on! It's for BLESMA. You have that leg off and the cash we raise will go straight to you.

ALI Well we'd better come up with something better than "Grand Old Duke of York" then, hadn't we? 'Cos last time

I checked a top of the range C leg cost more than fucking fifty pee.

FRANK *inserts a DVD into his laptop and starts working.*

ROGER Sixty grand. That's what I heard. Same as a Javelin missile.

JOHN I took out a Tali with one of those once. Fucking pink mist, mate, pink mist.

ALI That, my friend, is the power of economics. They pay a farmer ten dollars to take pot shots at you, and you fucking obliterate him with sixty grand's worth of missile.

ROGER All's fair, like they say.

CHARLIE In war maybe. Not in fucking love.

ALI You're not still bleating about your missus, are you?

CHARLIE Yeah, I am actually. You got a problem with that?

DARREN I'm telling you, you're better off without. Mine fucked off before I got back. I wasn't even injured yet. They look nice enough, but they're all fucking nuts. Not that I ever *saw* that much of her. Which was a bit ironic seeing as she worked for Ann Summers. Had sex toys coming out of my ears, but no sex. Three double penetrators but no one to fucking penetrate.

A **NURSE** *enters. She carries a clipboard.*

NURSE Anyone still want to sign up for kayaking down the Amazon?

JOHN Can't. Rowing the Atlantic.

FRANK Kilimanjaro.

NURSE Come on guys, any volunteers?

ALI, **JOHN**, **ROGER** *and* **SIMI** *exit. The* **NURSE** *exits.*

In the brief quiet we hear **CHRIS** *on the phone.* **DARREN** *begins to fall asleep.* **LEROY** *enters.*

CHRIS It's blue. On the top. There's a go faster stripe down the side? No, I'm not a patient here, I'm a… I'm a mentor. For the, er, Not Forgotten Association.

LEROY Mentor? More like a fucking mentalist! Weren't doing much mentoring last night, were you?

CHRIS Fuck off.

CHRIS *gives* **LEROY** *the finger as he hangs up and looks up another number from his screen and begins to dial.*

CHARLIE *has taken the sock off his stump and is massaging his scar.*

LEROY How come your stump's so fucking Gucci?

CHARLIE Gucci? What's so fucking Gucci about my stump?

LEROY The scar. Yours is well neat. Mine's like a fucking arse.

He rolls up his trouser leg.

Look, it's got bum cheeks and everything. I could fart out of this fucker.

CHARLIE You should get some ink on that.

He looks at it more closely.

I mean, I was going to make mine a shark's mouth. But that. You're half way to a whole face there. Or even a knob. Do you still feel yours?

LEROY My knob?

CHARLIE No! Your legs.

LEROY Yeah. Not always, but sometimes. If I sit on the floor it feels like my legs are going *through* the floor. It's weird.

CHARLIE I get this itch in my ankle. The one that isn't there anymore? Drives me fucking mad. Feels like my whole leg is in a really thick ski boot.

CHRIS It's Nike. Yeah, Nike.

LEROY Charlie, you been offered much porn work?

CHARLIE What?

LEROY Porn. Since you lost your leg? You been offered any work?

CHARLIE Er, no?

Beat.

Why, have you?

LEROY Yeah. Loads.

CHARLIE Really?

LEROY Yeah. Must be a double amputee thing, I guess.

CHARLIE That's sick.

Beat.

You ever do it?

LEROY Went along once. But, nah. Didn't follow through. The chick was proper fat. And she had this weird birthmark.

CHARLIE Er, right. And of course you're fucking Tom Cruise.

LEROY You'd be surprised. Women love this. They do.

CHRIS Hello. Is that the White Horse? I was just wondering if you'd found a leg... It's blue, on the top. It's got a trainer on it. Nike... OK, thanks.

CHRIS hangs up.

CHARLIE Chris, what the fuck are you doing? You sound like Cinderella.

CHRIS Trying to find my fucking leg, aren't I?

LEROY Where'd you last see it?

CHRIS In the Black Lion, I think. Yeah.

He points to FRANK.

You was drinking out of it!

FRANK Was I?

CHARLIE Actually, now I come to think of it, yeah, you were. Snakebite and black.

FRANK Nice.

CHRIS Yeah, great. But now I've only got one fucking leg for the weekend, in't I?

LEROY What you doing over there, Frank?

FRANK Editing Jonesy's tapes, innit?

CHARLIE Jonesy? Forty two Commando? Killed same day as Steve Owens?

FRANK Yeah.

LEROY Why you editing them?

FRANK His mum found them in his stuff when it was sent back. She wants me to put them onto DVD, so she can watch them. So now I've got to fucking edit them all, haven't I?

CHARLIE Why?

FRANK 'Cos half of them is him saying he loves his mum, what it's like in Afghan an' that. But then the other half's this stuff.

FRANK *presses play. The sounds of two people having sex.* FRANK *shows the laptop to* CHARLIE *and* CHRIS.

CHARLIE Jesus fucking Christ!

LEROY She's wearing his beret!

CHRIS *joins them. As one they all turn their heads to the side, until they are horizontal to the screen.*

ALL Fuck!

*A **DELIVERY MAN** enters, holding a pair of mannequins' legs.*

DELIVERY MAN Er, anyone know where I'm putting these?

FRANK, CHARLIE, CHRIS *and* **LEROY** *all look up at him. For a moment they stare at him, the sound of Jonesy having sex still coming from the computer.*

LEROY Are you taking the piss?

DELIVERY MAN Sorry?

CHARLIE What the fuck?

The **DELIVERY MAN** *looks down at his docket.*

DELIVERY MAN This is er...?

A **NURSE** *enters, carrying the body of a mannequin. It wears a Team GB lycra top.*

NURSE Yes, it is. Thanks, I'll sign for those.

To the **SOLDIERS**.

Perhaps we can let Jonesy rest in peace now?

FRANK *turns off the volume.*

(to the **DELIVERY MAN***)* Just through here please, for the Paralympics display. Thanks.

The **DELIVERY MAN** *goes to exit. As he passes,* **CHARLIE** *takes one of the legs.*

CHARLIE You won't be needing this. It's for the *para* Olympics?

The **DELIVERY MAN** *shrugs and exits with just the one leg.*

(handing the leg to **CHRIS***)* Here you go, Cinders. Until you track down your glass slipper.

CHRIS Fucking great, thanks.

A **NURSE** *enters.*

NURSE Corporal Fowler?

CHARLIE Yes, mam! You come to take me away from this tea party?

She hands him a package.

NURSE This came for you. *(to* **ALL***)* Meds in two minutes!

ALI enters with the rest of the group who left.

ALI Thank fuck for that.

CHARLIE *pulls out a rectangular piece of metal from his package.*

CHARLIE Sweet! Take a look at that, motherfuckers.

He turns the object around to reveal a personalised numberplate. NO LEG 14.

The group nod in approval.

ROGER Herrick fourteen?

CHARLIE Yeah.

JOHN What you got coming?

CHARLIE BMW. Three series. Black. If I'd lost a nut or the other leg I'd have gone for a Merc, but you know, needs must.

ALI I swear, it's getting like a footballer's driveway round here. What is it with you lot and the cars?

LEROY Motobility isn't it? You have that leg off and you'll qualify too.

ALI Don't joke mate. I've been thinking about it. I mean I'm still in this wheelchair when other blokes with one leg are up and climbing fucking Everest. I mean, what?

LEROY Just watch out for the small talk, that's all I'd say.

ALI What?

LEROY I'm not kidding. It's the worst thing about it. You wheel into a room and you can bet some regimental old duffer will clock you and think, "Oh, young bloke, no legs, I'll go and talk to him." It's like, I just want a drink, or some food, but I can't because I'm too busy passing the time of day with Colonel Blimp about having no fucking legs.

Three **NURSES** *enter carrying trays of medication.*

ROGER Eh up! Make room for the cavalry.

They begin going about the room, handing out the medication.

ALI AND ROGER *(singing)*
AND WHEN THEY WERE UP THEY WERE UP,
AND WHEN THEY WERE DOWN THEY WERE DOWN
AND WHEN THEY WERE ONLY HALFWAY UP—

DARREN *is woken by the singing.*

DARREN They were neither up nor down.

ALI Wahey, the Kraken awakes! Welcome back, Sobey, my son!

The **NURSES** *reach the group. As they hand them their medication they begin singing.*

[MUSIC 04: "PHARMACOPEIA"]

NURSES *(sung)*
CODEINE, TRAMADOL, FENTANYL, ORAMORPH,
  PARACETEMOL, MST.
AMITRIPTYLINE, DIAZAPAM, MIRTAZAPINE, CITALOPRAM,
RANITIDINE, OMEPRAZOLE, LACTULOSE, BUTRAN,
  IBUPROFEN.
VENLAFAXINE, COCODOMOL.

COMPANY
CODEINE, TRAMADOL, FENTANYL, ORAMORPH,
  PARACETEMOL, MST.
AMITRIPTYLINE, DIAZAPAM, MIRTAZAPINE, CITALOPRAM,

RANITIDINE, OMEPRAZOLE, LACTULOSE, BUTRAN, IBUPROFEN.
VENLAFAXINE, COCODOMOL.

(Four Groups sing as a round)

CODEINE, TRAMADOL, FENTANYL, ORAMORPH, PARACETEMOL, MST.
AMITRIPTYLINE, DIAZAPAM, MIRTAZAPINE, CITALOPRAM,
RANITIDINE, OMEPRAZOLE, LACTULOSE, BUTRAN, IBUPROFEN.
VENLAFAXINE, COCODOMOL.

COMPANY
KETAMINE!

The lights fade down on the repeating song.

Scene Six – Someone To Hold

Blackout.

Lights up on the **PSYCHOLOGIST** *talking to* **CHARLIE**. *As they talk the silhouette of a Vallon man sweeping for I.E.D.s is seen upstage.*

PSYCHOLOGIST ...Severe allergic reactions; disorientation; excessive sweating; fainting; fast or irregular heartbeat; fever; hallucinations; loss of coordination; mental or mood changes; agitation; depression; red, swollen, blistered or peeling skin, and... seizures.

CHARLIE Severe nausea? Vomiting, diarrhoea; headaches; suicidal thoughts – 'cos I need more of those right? – loss of appetite; tiredness; weakness; pale shit and dark piss.

Beat.

And I mean, that's just the tramadol. Wait 'til you hear about the venlafaxine—

PSYCHOLOGIST It's OK, Charlie. I see your point. The meds aren't helping?

CHARLIE No. The drugs, as the song says, don't fucking work. I mean, yeah, they *work*, but at the same time they mess everything up.

PSYCHOLOGIST Like?

CHARLIE Sleep. Attention. Anger. Sex.

PSYCHOLOGIST How are things with Lauren?

Beat.

CHARLIE I don't know. Answer me this, doc? How can you be angry at someone for loving you too much? She'll try and help me, or cuddle me – oh, yeah, cuddling, that's the worst – and I'll be like. Get the fuck off me!

PSYCHOLOGIST You've lost interest in sex?

CHARLIE No. Yes. I mean… you get back and you *think* what you want is a slut. It is. You think you'll want to do all that stuff you've been dreaming about doing for six fucking months in the desert. But when you *do* get back, you don't. You don't. The juices aren't flowing. Not the *actual* juices, no problem there – but you know, the metaphorical ones. You want something else instead.

PSYCHOLOGIST And what's that? What do you want?

CHARLIE Exactly what she's offering. That closeness, the contact. But when she does. There's this fucking distance and I just want to be alone. On my own.

CHRIS enters and approaches the PSYCHOLOGIST.

CHRIS She doesn't understand. She thinks I'm a lazy bastard. I know she does. She gives me these fucking chores, these lists. And then the meds knock me out. And what the kids say. That's the worst. "Daddy, are you drunk?" "Why is Daddy sleeping all the time?"

PSYCHOLOGIST Have you tried explaining things to them?

CHRIS Like what? How every time I see them I think of those kids in Afghan? No. I've put my bed in the back room now. So they don't have to see me like this.

PSYCHOLOGIST And your wife? How's she coping?

CHRIS Don't get me wrong. I know how hard it's been for her. They've all had to get on without me. And that's part of the problem – they've got their own routines now. Without me. They live without me.

Beat.

Do you know what she said the other day? "Chris didn't come back." That's what she said. "The Chris that went away hasn't come back." And in a way she's right. She is.

FRANK *enters and approaches the* **PSYCHOLOGIST**.

FRANK I'll just go out on the piss all day. Don't give a fuck, then I'll get wound up by something small and I'll just want to smash something up. Or someone.

PSYCHOLOGIST Only when you drink?

FRANK Well, the drink makes it worse. The anger's there all the time. And these images. Like, I don't fucking know. When an I.E.D blew my mates hands off. The look in his eyes. That kind of thing.

PSYCHOLOGIST You're on probation now right?

FRANK Yeah. But they said if I come and talk to you, it'll keep me out of prison.

PSYCHOLOGIST Does that worry Michelle? You going away again? Doing time?

FRANK Yeah, yeah it does.

Beat.

I don't know. When she's talking to me. When I can't be near her. I just want to go back there, get vengeance on the fuckers who done this to me. It's like… It's like there's hatred running through my whole body. But I do love her. I do.

CHRIS She's right. She is.

CHARLIE She's pretty amazing doc. I mean, I know she's my solution. But I'm fucking it up. And it's like I can't stop.

As he continues the three women, **LAUREN**, **MARIE** *and* **MICHELLE** *(carrying a child) enter and come to stand beside the three men.*

It's like I really, really want to square this one away but I can't. It's a whole second tour doc. It is. The one no one tells you about. I mean, I'll storm a fucking compound tomorrow. Even with one fucking leg. But *this* tour.

I'm outnumbered. You take meds for the pain, then meds for the meds. Then every time you close your eyes...

The **PSYCHOLOGIST** *exits.*

And the casualties. That's what's so fucked up. They're the very people you always said you'd fight for. The ones you said you'd protect. The ones you love.

CHARLIE *reaches a hand out towards* **LAUREN**. *She takes off her engagement ring and places it in his palm, then turns away.*

CHRIS *reaches towards* **MARIE**. *She stares at him as if she doesn't know him, then places a child's toy in his hand before turning away.*

FRANK *reaches towards* **MICHELLE**. *She looks at the baby, then at him, then turns away.*

The three women exit, followed by **CHRIS** *and* **FRANK**.

Music in the style of Anthony and the Johnson's ["**HOPE THERE'S SOMEONE**"*] is played*.*

CHRIS *and* **LEROY** *enter to join* **CHARLIE** *in a wheelchair dance. The three women enter to join them.*

As the **DANCERS** *exit* **JOHN** *appears in close up, projected on the screen.*

JOHN *(on screen)* My Mum, bless her, she quit her job to stay with me. She'd be trying to care for me, and I'd be like,

---

* A licence to produce THE TWO WORLDS OF CHARLIE F. does not include a performance licence for "HOPE THERE'S SOMEONE". The publisher and author suggest that the licensee contact PRS to ascertain the music publisher and contact such music publisher to license or acquire permission for performance of the song. If a licence or permission is unattainable for "HOPE THERE'S SOMEONE", the licensee may not use the song in THE TWO WORLDS OF CHARLIE F. but should create an original composition in a similar style or use a similar song in the public domain. For further information, please see Music Use Note on page iii.

really snappy, telling her to fuck off, go away. Then straight away I'd think 'why did I do that?' It's weird, you want it, you do. But then you'll be a twat, and tell them to fuck off. It's like being two people.

But she's amazing, she is. She's always been there, when I needed her. I'd go out on the piss, and she'd find me later, in her kitchen, fucking laughing at YouTube clips of I.E.Ds. Just going crazy. Then ten minutes later, I'd be in her arms, crying. She's had to put up with so much. But she's always supported me, always.

Fade to black.

Scene Seven – Enemy Territory

Speeches by **DANIEL** *and* **CHRIS** *are projected onto the stage.*

DANIEL How I think of it is, I've got my old brain, and my new brain. My old brain was the one that evolved for the first thirty eight years of my life. It was me. My new brain, that's the one I was given when I was blown up. I mean, in an instant, I became a different person. And people don't always understand. When I say my brain hurts, or I have trouble thinking, or that I get really tired they'll say "oh yeah, I get that sometimes too." It's frustrating, because I don't like the new me. I don't always recognise myself, and they just don't understand.

CHRIS I call it "stump jump", these sudden spasms and shocks, like I've touched a car battery with the end of my stump. I've found vodka and Ibuprofen's a good cure for that. But then there's the phantom pain too – ten thousand volts going through legs you don't have. A lit match stuck under my toenail, burning for days. It's the frustration that breeds the anger though, as much as the pain. When I first got home from the hospital I tried to build a kennel for my dog. A flat-pack thing it was, but I couldn't fucking do it could I? Couldn't even build a fucking kennel. I ended up taking a hammer to it in the end, smashed it to pieces all over the lawn.

Lights come up to reveal **CHARLIE**, *wearing his prosthetic leg and a pair of shorts.*

CHARLIE You know what my nickname was in the Corps? Foxtrot. And no, not for my fancy fucking footwork either. Charlie Fowler. C.F. – In NATO phonetics, "Charlie Foxtrot". In army and navy slang – "Clusterfuck". "A situation disintergrating in every direction at once." I won't lie to you, for a while there, after this happened, I *became* my nickname. I mean, I was a fucking mess. And I wasn't alone. There's the denial phase, the "sitting on your ass playing Xbox pissing everyone off" phase, the meds, the pain... But we're soldiers, you know. What do they teach us in training? Adapt and overcome. And that's what you do, eventually.

Beat.

In the end, for me, there were two things that really made that happen. The first was realising that just like you fight for your mates, your boys, out there, on the ground, so you can fight for them here too. It might be just a phonecall, an email, dropping round. But you can look out for each other *here* just like you did on tour. I mean, whenever we pushed into new areas in Afghan, we went as a patrol didn't we? And it's the same here. When we push into that uncharted territory, as much as possible, we do so *together*. Oh, yeah, the second thing? Well... actually, you know what? You're about to hear about that now anyway.

As **CHARLIE** *walks upstage lights come up to reveal a lapdancing club. Two backlit screens show the silhouettes of two* **DANCERS**. *A* **WAITRESS** *is taking a drinks order from two* **BUSINESSMEN**. **ROGER, ALI, JOHN, SIMI** *and* **DARREN** *all enter to join* **CHARLIE**.

ALI Charlie Boy! What's your poison?

CHARLIE Beer. Thanks man.

JOHN Are we all here?

DANIEL Er, yeah. Aren't we? I thought I counted everyone off...

ALI Jesus! Who put the guy with the neuro injury in charge of numbers?

DANIEL I could have sworn...

LEROY *enters.*

LEROY Great, thanks for that lads. Had to be carried up by tweedle dee and tweedle dum didn't I?

*The two **DANCERS** come out from behind the screen and begin to mingle among the **SOLDIERS** as the **WAITRESS** takes drinks orders.*

DANCER 1 Hello love. You interested in a private dance?

LEROY Er, yeah, I guess so. Is it a lapdance?

She looks at his legs.

DANCER 1 Well, it's hardly going to be a waltz is it darling? Yes, it's a lap dance.

LEROY That's lucky, 'cos a lap's all I got!

LEROY *and* **DANCER 1** *go behind the screens.*

ALI Alright darling?

WAITRESS Evening sir.

ALI You know what a fat penguin does?

WAITRESS I'm sorry?

ALI Breaks the ice! Get it? Breaks the ice...

*The two **BUSINESSMEN** approach **CHARLIE** and **CHRIS**.*

BUSINESSMAN 1 Alright lads? Having a good night?

BUSINESSMAN 2 Are you all, er veterans then? Is that it?

CHARLIE Well, some of us are still serving. We're soldiers but, yeah.

BUSINESSMAN 1 Well I think you do a fantastic job. Really. People don't recognise it enough.

BUSINESSMAN 2 I've got a friend who was in the army.

CHARLIE Right. Great.

BUSINESSMAN 1 Look, will you let us get you all a round. Please. It would be our pleasure.

CHARLIE No, honestly, you're alright mate.

ALI Shut up Charlie. Jack and Coke please mate, cheers!

BUSINESSMAN 2 Waitress! Waitress! A round for these lads please. On us.

BUSINESSMAN 1 So, have you been overseas?

CHARLIE Yeah

BUSINESSMAN 2 Iraq was it?

CHARLIE Afghan.

BUSINESSMAN 1 Wow. Really? So you've seen some action then?

CHARLIE *and* **CHRIS** *look at their missing legs.*

CHARLIE Er, Yeah? A bit.

CHRIS Some.

BUSINESSMAN 2 Did you kill any?

CHARLIE Sorry?

BUSINESSMAN 1 I think what he's asking is whether you killed anyone over there?

Beat.

Did you?

CHARLIE Er, I don't really want to –

BUSINESSMAN 2 How many? Do you know?

CHRIS Look –

BUSINESSMAN 1 I imagine it'd be hard to tell? From what I hear you don't often see them do you?

ROGER *joins the group.*

ROGER Look, mate, thanks for the drinks and everything, but do you mind not asking those kind of questions?

BUSINESSMAN 2 Oh. Oh, I'm sorry.

BUSINESSMAN 1 We didn't mean to cause offence. Sorry.

BUSINESSMAN 2 Are you with them too?

ROGER Them? Who the fuck is them?

BUSINESSMAN 2 The soldiers.

ROGER Yeah. I am.

BUSINESSMAN 2 So... I mean, sorry, but what's wrong with you?

ROGER I don't know, I broke my back in two places, had discs at C4 and C5 replaced, I'm addicted to meds and sometimes the pain is so bad I collapse and piss myself in public. What's wrong with you?

DARREN and JOHN come over.

JOHN Alright Rog, take it easy

The BUSINESSMEN back off.

BUSINESSMAN 2 Right. OK. Fine.

ROGER Prick.

DANCER 2 approaches CHARLIE. She wears a NURSE's outfit.

DANCER 2 Hello. It's Charlie isn't it?

CHARLIE Oh god, you know my name. Have I really been here that much?

DANCER 2 Once or twice. Look, would you like a private dance?

CHARLIE Er, thanks, but I'm fine. Thanks.

DANCER 2 Really? Even if I say please?

CHARLIE Well, no. Honestly, that's sweet, but...

BUSINESSMAN 1 Take the dance. It's on us. Please.

ALI If you don't want it Charlie I'll have it!

DANCER 2 Please?

CHARLIE OK, OK, I'll have the dance.

The screens move to isolate **CHARLIE** *and* **DANCER 2**.

CHARLIE Look, I'll be honest, I'm not really in the mood for this.

DANCER 2 It's alright. I didn't really want to give you a dance.

CHARLIE Oh. Then why – ?

DANCER 2 Because I wanted to give you something else.

CHARLIE Oh, right. Well, Jesus. That's really kind of you. I mean, I know everyone's getting into this "help for heroes" stuff, but –

DANCER 2 Whose Lauren?

Beat.

CHARLIE Sorry?

DANCER 2 Lauren? Who is she?

CHARLIE How do you know –?

DANCER 2 When you've been in before. When you get drunk. You start talking about her. A lot.

CHARLIE I do? Yeah, I guess that happens.

DANCER 2 And that tat on your arm. I'm guessing it used to say her name?

CHARLIE Yeah. Yeah it did. Before the frag and the scars fucked it up. Guess I should have known then eh?

DANCER 2 Known what?

CHARLIE She's my fiancée… She *was* my fiancée.

DANCER 2 Oh. Bollocks. I'm sorry.

CHARLIE Not your fault. Not hers either. All mine.

DANCER 2 I guess you might not want this now then.

CHARLIE Want what?

DANCER 2 This.

She hands him a folded piece of paper.

CHARLIE What is it?

DANCER 2 Well, I've seen you've all got tattoos. You all seem to like tats.

CHARLIE Yeah, everyone likes a bit of ink.

DANCER 2 So I designed a new one for you. I've gone back to college. It's meant to be, well, I thought you might like a new one.

CHARLIE "Lauren".

DANCER 2 Yeah, but I understand if –

CHARLIE It's beautiful.

DANCER 2 You can change the words underneath if you want. And the name now I guess!

CHARLIE "But love survives the venom of the snake."

DANCER 2 It's from this poem we're studying. It's by a soldier, but, like I said –

CHARLIE It's perfect. Thank you.

Beat.

DANCER 2 Is it really over?

CHARLIE I don't know.

DANCER 2 'Cos the way you talk about her. When –

CHARLIE I know. I know.

DANCER 2 Look, I'm going to have to go. The manager gets in a right strop if we're in here too long. But, well, like I said. I wanted to give you something. Sorry if it's –

CHARLIE I meant what I said. It's perfect. Thank you.

She leans in and gives him a peck on the cheek, then exits. The lights stay up on **CHARLIE**.

Scene Eight – Leaving

CHARLIE "But love survives the venom of the snake." When you're discharged from the services one of the last things you do is hand over your I.D. Your identity. It's a death, of sorts. At least, it certainly feels like a kind of grief, afterwards. A mourning. For the loss of that bond. For the family you'd joined, lived with, fought with, but are now being asked to leave.

It feels sudden. One day you're in. The next you're out. But it isn't. It's a slow process. A process of departure. And that's one of the problems. It takes seconds to hand over that I.D. But it can take years to remove the uniform.

We do have to take it off though, one day. The stories of our injuries all began with an engagement of some kind. A contact. And they're only going to be brought to an end with another kind of contact. Another kind of engagement –

He looks at the tattoo design.

– or re-engagement. But you can't do that if you're still wearing your uniform.

It's OK though. Because it isn't just about leaving is it? It's about joining too, right? I mean all of us here, yeah we're leaving the services, but we're also joining the oldest regiment there is. The regiment of the wounded. It's a regiment with an illustrious history that goes back to the earliest days of mankind. You might not be familiar with all of its victories, but believe me it has thousands to its name. Millions. And its winning them every day. In hospitals, on the streets, in bedrooms and living rooms.

He taps his head.

In here.

The rest of the cast enter upstage and begin walking downstage to join **CHARLIE**.

The regimental rank and file are recruited from all over the world. Britain. America. Africa. Iraq. Afghanistan. Men. Women. Children. And it's growing. Even now, as we speak, it's growing. And until we stop fighting, its going to keep on growing. And its deploying too. Every day. Not to a battlefield, or to a base. But to you. To out there. We've all been training for that deployment. We've been getting ready, and now we *are* ready. So we hope you are too. Because we don't live in two worlds do we? We live in one.

Beat.

And don't you ever forget it.

Fade to black.

ABOUT THE AUTHOR

Owen Sheers has written two collections of poetry, *The Blue Book* and *Skirrid Hill*. His non-fiction includes *The Dust Diaries* and *Calon: A Journey to the Heart of Welsh Rugby*. His debut novel, *Resistance*, has been translated into ten languages and was made into a film in 2011. His plays include *The Passion*, *Mametz* and *The Two Worlds of Charlie F.*, which won the Amnesty International Freedom of Expression award. His verse drama *Pink Mist* won Welsh Book of the Year and was staged in Bristol and London by Bristol Old Vic. His second novel, *I Saw a Man*, was shortlisted for the Prix Femina étranger. His writing for TV includes the BAFTA nominated *The Green Hollow* and *To Provide All People*. He has been a NYPL Cullman Fellow, Writer in Residence for the Wordsworth Trust and Artist in Residence for the Welsh Rugby Union. He is currently Professor in Creativity at Swansea University.

**Other plays by OWEN SHEERS
published and licensed by Concord Theatricals**

Mametz

Pink Mist

Unicorns, Almost

www.ingramcontent.com/pod-product-compliance
Ingram Content Group UK Ltd.
Pitfield, Milton Keynes, MK11 3LW, UK
UKHW021907060225
454771UK00026B/488